MARC HELGESEN AND STEVEN

Active Listening

INTRODUCING

Skills for Understanding

Student's Book

CAMBRIDGE
UNIVERSITY PRESS

To our parents, Ken and Esther Helgesen and Curt and Clara Brown,
who, when we were younger, often reminded us: *Listen*!

Published by the Press Syndicate of the University of Cambridge
The Pitt Building, Trumpington Street, Cambridge CB2 1RP
40 West 20th Street, New York, NY 10011-4211, USA
10 Stamford Road, Oakleigh, Melbourne 3166, Australia

© Cambridge University Press 1995

First published 1995

Printed in the United States of America

Library of Congress Cataloging-in-Publication Data
has been applied for.

A catalog record for this book is available from the British Library

ISBN 0-521-39881-9   Student's Book
ISBN 0-521-39884-3   Teacher's Manual
ISBN 0-521-39887-8   Cassettes

Book design; layout and design services: Six West Design

Illustrators:
Adventure House
Daisy de Puthod
Randy Jones
Wally Neibart
Six West Design
Andrew Toos
Sam Viviano

Contents

Plan of Book

	Topics/ Functions	Listening Skills	Grammar/ Vocabulary
Before you begin: **Learn how to listen**	Explaining types of listening	Listening for the main idea Listening for specific information Listening "between the lines"	
Unit 1: **Meeting new people**	Meeting people	Choosing appropriate responses Understanding personal information questions	Yes-no questions (present of *be* and simple present)
Unit 2: **Brothers and sisters**	Discussing family relationships	Understanding descriptions of people Following directions	Possessive adjectives Simple present Family words
Unit 3: **Numbers**	Asking for and giving (numerical) information	Understanding and processing numbers Understanding sports scores	Numbers
Unit 4: **Let's eat!**	Talking about food and places to eat	Inferring topics Understanding suggestions	*Let's . . .* Names of foods
Unit 5: **Your free time**	Talking about free-time activities	Identifying frequency Confirming and revising predictions	Frequency adverbs
Unit 6: **That's a nice shirt.**	Giving opinions about and describing clothing	Understanding descriptions of clothing Understanding reasons	Descriptive adjectives Clothing words
Unit 7: **Furniture and houses**	Describing things in a house and what they are for	Inferring topics Understanding descriptions of things	Simple present for descriptions Names of furniture and rooms in a house
Unit 8: **How do you start** **your day?**	Talking about routines	Identifying routines Understanding questions about activities	Simple present Sequence markers Simple past
Unit 9: **I'd like to see that!**	Giving opinions about movies	Understanding responses Inferring kinds of movies Understanding evaluations	Movie genres
Unit 10: **Where is it?**	Describing location and giving directions	Following directions Identifying locations	Imperatives Prepositions of location

	Topics/ Functions	Listening Skills	Grammar/ Vocabulary
Unit 11: *The Midnight* *Special*	Enjoying a folk song	Understanding a song Identifying a sequence of events Identifying word stress	Word stress
Unit 12: **Gifts and greetings**	Describing gifts and greetings in different countries	Identifying reasons Identifying customs	Negative imperatives (*Don't . . .*) *You shouldn't . . .*
Unit 13: **Time changes** **everything.**	Talking about what people did when they were younger	Identifying jobs Understanding personal information questions	Past with *used to* Names of jobs and occupations
Unit 14: **Can you describe it?**	Describing people, things, and events	Understanding descriptions of people and things Understanding descriptions of events	Descriptive adjectives
Unit 15: **Languages**	Talking about the languages of the world	Identifying countries Distinguishing types of English	American and British vocabulary and pronunciation differences
Unit 16: **I like that!**	Discussing likes and dislikes	Identifying preferences Understanding instructions	Infinitives (*to* + verb) and gerunds (verb + *-ing*)
Unit 17: **Strange news**	Evaluating newspaper headlines and stories	Understanding newspaper headlines Understanding summaries Evaluating information	Simple past
Unit 18: **Holidays**	Talking about holidays and customs in different countries	Identifying dates Identifying events	Present tenses: present of *be* and simple present for descriptions
Unit 19: **Inventions**	Describing inventions and where they came from	Understanding specific information Identifying the purpose of something	Infinitive of purpose: (*You can* *use it to . . .*)
Unit 20: **Folktales**	Appreciating folktales	Identifying a sequence of events Understanding and enjoying a story	Simple past

Acknowledgments

Illustrations

Adventure House   34, 36 (top), 48/49, 68/69
Daisy de Puthod   16, 24, 25, 26, 50, 60/61
Randy Jones   14, 17, 19, 23, 31, 35, 38, 39, 42, 47, 54, 65
Wally Neibart   3, 5, 10, 15, 18, 22, 29, 30, 33 (bottom), 52, 57, 58, 63, 64
Six West Design   21 (bottom), 33 (top)
Andrew Toos   4, 9, 20, 27, 36, 40, 46, 51, 62
Sam Viviano   6, 21 (top), 37, 41

Photographic credits

The authors and publisher are grateful for permission to reproduce the following photographs.

6   (*from left to right*) © The Stock Market/Roy Morsch; © The Stock Market/Michael A. Keller, 1992; © Douglas Bryant/FPG International Corp.
7   (*from top to bottom*) © Jim Cummins/FPG International Corp.; © The Stock Market/Paul Barton, 1990
13   (*clockwise from top*) © Telegraph Colour Library/FPG International Corp.; © The Stock Market/José Fuste, 1994; © James Blank/FPG International Corp.; © Russell Cheyne/Tony Stone Worldwide; © The Stock Market/Tibor Bognár, 1991; © Telegraph Colour/FPG International Corp.
28   (*clockwise from top*) © The Stock Market/Naideau, 1992; © The Stock Market/Jon Feingersh, 1989; © Telegraph Colour Library/FPG International Corp.; © J. DeSelliers/Superstock
32   (*from left to right*) © The Stock Market/Jose L. Pelaez, 1993; © P. R. Productions/Superstock
43   (*clockwise from top*) © Greg Gorman/Liaison International; © Benainous Duclos/Liaison International; © Liaison Distribution/Liaison International; © Steve Allen/Liaison International; © Steve Allen/Liaison International; © FPG International Corp.; © Frederic Reclain/Liaison International; © Kip Rano/Liaison International; © Berliner Studio/Liaison International
44   (*from left to right*) © The Stock Market/Gabe Palmer, 1990; © Ron Rovtar/FPG International Corp.; © Jade Albert/FPG International Corp.
59   (*clockwise from top*) © The Stock Market/Roy Morsch; © Telegraph Colour Library/FPG International Corp.; © Tourism Authority of Korea; © Tourism Authority of Thailand

Authors' acknowledgments

We would like to thank our **reviewers** for their helpful suggestions: Chuck Sandy and Dorolyn Smith.

We would also like to acknowledge the **students** and **teachers** in the following schools and institutes who piloted components of *Active Listening: Introducing Skills for Understanding:*

Alianza Cultural Uruguay-Estados Unidos, Montevideo, Uruguay; **Bae Centre,** Buenos Aires, Argentina; **Bunka Institute of Foreign Languages,** Tokyo, Japan; **Chin-Yi Institute of Technology,** Taichung City, Taiwan; **Educational Options,** Santa Clara, California, USA; **Impact English,** Santiago, Chile; **Instituto Cultural de Idiomas Ltda.,** Caxias do Sul, Brazil; **Kansai University of Foreign Studies,** Osaka, Japan; **Koyo Shoji Co. Ltd.,** Hitachi, Japan; **Osaka Institute of Technology,** Osaka, Japan; **Southern Illinois University,** Niigata, Japan; **Suzugamine Women's College,** Hiroshima City, Japan; **Tokyo Foreign Language College,** Tokyo, Japan; **Umeda Business College,** Osaka, Japan; **University of Michigan English Language Institute,** Ann Arbor, Michigan, USA.

Thanks also go to Hey Chang, Gerald Couzens, Betsy Davis, Marion Delarche, Carl Dusthimer, David Fisher, Yoko Futami, Robin Guenzel, Yoko Hakuta, Brenda Hayashi, Patricia Hunt, J.R. Kim, Sean Lewis, Michael McLaughlin, Steven Maginn, Lalitha Manuel, Lionel Menasche, Lisa Minetti, Christine O'Neill, Ruth Owen, Susan Ryan, John Smith, Serena Spenser, Noriko Suzuki, Kazue Takahashi, Brian Tomlinson, Paul Wadden, and Michiko Wako.

Finally, a special thanks to the editors and advisors at Cambridge University Press: Suzette André, Colin Bethell, Mary Carson, Riitta da Costa, Kyoko Fukunaga, Deborah Goldblatt, John Haywood, Jinsook Kim, Stephanie Karras, Koen Van Landeghem, Kathy Niemczyk, Helen Sandiford, Kumiko Sekioka, and Mary Vaughn.

To the student

Welcome to *Active Listening: Introducing Skills for Understanding*. We hope this book will help you learn to listen to English more effectively. You will practice listening to English. At the same time, you'll learn "how to listen." That is, you'll learn to make use of the English you already know. You'll also think about your reasons for listening. When you do that, listening and understanding become much easier.

This book has twenty units. Each unit has five parts:

- **Warming Up** Warming Up activities will help you remember what you know about the unit topic. This is an important step. It helps you get ready for listening.
- **Listening Task 1** You will listen to people in many different situations. Sometimes you'll listen for specific information such as numbers and places. Other times, you'll have to use what you hear to figure out things that aren't said directly. For example, you'll need to decide how strongly people feel about things they like and dislike.
- **Culture Corner** This is a short reading. It gives information about the unit topic.
- **Listening Task 2** Listening Task 2 is on the same theme as Listening Task 1, but it is a little more challenging.
- **Your Turn to Talk** This is a speaking activity. You will use the language you have just heard. You will do this task in pairs or small groups.

Listening tips

- Why are you listening? Ask yourself, "What do I need to know? What do I need to do?" You will listen to many kinds of language and do many kinds of tasks. You will need to listen in different ways. These ways are explained in the first unit, "Before You Begin." In Units 1–20, each listening task has a box at the top of the page. The box tells you the purpose of the activity.
- The tapes that go with the book are very natural. You won't be able to understand every word you hear. That's OK. You don't need to. Listen for the general meaning.
- Don't worry about words you don't know. Many students look up every new word in their dictionaries. Here's an idea: When you hear a new word, just listen. When you hear it a second time, try to guess the meaning. When you hear it a third time and still don't understand, then look it up in your dictionary.

We hope you enjoy using this book, and we hope you learn to be a better, more active listener.

To the teacher

Active Listening: Introducing Skills for Understanding is a course for high-beginning to low-intermediate students of North American English. As the name implies, the course recognizes that listening is a very active process. Learners bring knowledge to the class and perform a wide variety of interactive tasks. *Active Listening* can be used as the main text for listening classes or as a supplement in speaking or integrated skills classes.

ABOUT THE BOOK

The book includes twenty units, each with a warm-up activity; two main listening tasks; Culture Corner, a reading passage that presents information related to the unit theme; and Your Turn to Talk, a short speaking activity done in pairs or small groups. In addition, there is an introductory lesson called "Before You Begin." This lesson introduces learning strategies and types of listening, including listening for gist and inference. The lesson is particularly useful for learners whose previous experience has been limited primarily to listening for specific information, or to answering literal comprehension questions.

The units can be taught in the order presented or out of sequence to follow the themes of the class or another book it is supplementing. In general, the tasks in the second half of the book are more challenging than those in the first.

Unit organization

Each unit begins with an activity called **Warming Up.** This activity, usually done in pairs, serves to remind learners of the language they already know. The tasks are designed to activate prior knowledge or "schemata." In the process of doing the warm-up activity, students work from their knowledge and, at the same time, use vocabulary and structures that are connected with a particular function or grammar point. The exercise makes the listening tasks it precedes easier because the learners are prepared.

Listening Task 1 and **Listening Task 2** are the major listening exercises. The tasks are balanced to include a variety of listening types including listening for gist, identifying specific information, and understanding inferences. The purpose of each task is identified in a box in the top-right corner of each page. Because *Active Listening* features a task-based approach, learners should be doing the activities as they listen, rather than waiting until they have finished listening to a particular segment. To make this easier, writing is kept to a minimum. In most cases, students check boxes, number items, or write only words or short phrases.

Culture Corner is a short reading passage on the theme of the unit. In most cases, you'll want to use it as homework or as a break in classroom routine. Each Culture Corner ends with one or two discussion questions.

Your Turn to Talk, the final section of each unit, is a short, fluency-oriented speaking task done in pairs or small groups. In general, corrections are not appropriate during these activities. However, you may want to note common mistakes and, at the end of the period, write them on the board. Encourage learners to correct themselves.

Hints and techniques

■ Be sure to do the Warming Up section for each unit. This preview can foster a very healthy learning strategy. It teaches the students "how to listen." Also, it makes students more successful, which, in turn, motivates and encourages them.

■ In general, you'll only want to play a particular segment one or two times. If the learners are still having difficulty, try telling them the answers. Then play the tape again and let them experience understanding what they heard.

■ If some students find listening very difficult, have them do the task in pairs, helping each other as necessary. The Teacher's Edition contains additional ideas.

■ Some students may not be used to active learning. Those learners may be confused by instructions since they are used to a more passive role. Explaining activities is usually the least effective way to give instructions. It is better to demonstrate. For example, give the instruction as briefly as possible (e.g., "Listen. Number the pictures."). Then play the first part of the tape. Stop the tape and elicit the correct answer from the learners. Those who weren't sure what to do will quickly understand. The same technique works for Warming Up and Your Turn to Talk. Lead one pair or group through the first step of the task. The other learners watch. They quickly see what they are supposed to do.

> *Active Listening: Introducing Skills for Understanding* is accompanied by a **Teacher's Edition** that contains a complete tapescript, step-by-step lesson plans, and expansion activities, as well as grammar and general notes.

HOW STUDENTS LEARN TO LISTEN

Many students find listening to be one of the most difficult skills in English. The following explains some of the ideas incorporated into the book to make students more effective listeners. *Active Listening: Introducing Skills for Understanding* is designed to help students make real and rapid progress. Recent research into teaching listening and its related receptive skill, reading, have given insights into how successful students learn foreign/second languages.

Bottom-up vs. top-down processing, a brick-wall analogy

To understand what our students are going through as they learn to listen or read, consider the "bottom-up vs. top-down processing" distinction. The distinction is based on the ways learners process and attempt to understand what they read or hear. With bottom-up processing, students start with the component parts: words, grammar, and the like. Top-down processing is the opposite. Students start from their background knowledge.

This might be better understood by means of a metaphor. Imagine a brick wall. If you are standing at the bottom looking at the wall brick by brick, you can easily see the details. It is difficult, however, to get an overall view of the wall. And, if you come to a missing brick (e.g., an unknown word or unfamiliar structure), you're stuck. If, on the other hand, you're sitting on the top of the wall, you can easily see the landscape. Of course, because of distance, you'll miss some details.

Students, particularly those with years of "classroom English" but little experience in really using the language, try to listen from the "bottom up."

They attempt to piece the meaning together, word by word. It is difficult for us, as native and advanced non-native English users, to experience what learners go through. However, try reading the following *from right to left*.

> word one ,slowly English process you When to easy is it ,now doing are you as ,time a at .word individual each of meaning the catch understand to difficult very is it ,However .passage the of meaning overall the

You were probably able to understand the paragraph:

> When you process English slowly, one word at a time, as you are doing now, it is easy to catch the meaning of each individual word. However, it is very difficult to understand the overall meaning of the passage.

While reading, however, it is likely you felt the frustration of bottom-up processing; you had to get each individual part before you could make sense of it. This is similar to what our students experience – and they're having to wrestle the meaning in a foreign language. Of course, this is an ineffective way to listen since it takes too long. While students are still trying to make sense of what has been said, the speaker keeps going. The students get lost.

Although their processing strategy is a negative, students do come to class with certain strengths. From their years of English study, most have a relatively large, if passive, vocabulary. They also often have a solid receptive knowledge of English grammar. We shouldn't neglect the years of life experience; our learners bring with them a wealth of background knowledge on many topics. These three strengths – vocabulary, grammar, and life experience – can be the tools for effective listening.

The Warming Up activities in *Active Listening* build on those strengths. By engaging the students in active, meaningful prelistening tasks, students integrate bottom-up and top-down processing. They start from meaning, but, in the process of doing the task, use vocabulary and structures (grammar) connected with the task, topic, or function. The result is an integrated listening strategy.

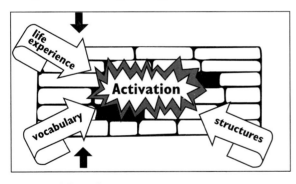

Types of listening

A second factor that is essential in creating effective listeners is exposing them to a variety of types of listening. Many students have only had experience with listening for literal comprehension. While listening for specific information is an important skill, it represents only one type. We have attempted to reach a balance in the book in order to give students experience with – and an understanding of – listening for gist and inference. Students usually are quick to understand the idea of listening for gist. They can easily imagine having to catch the general meaning of something they hear. Inference – listening "between the lines" – can be more difficult.

Take the following example (from the introductory unit, "Before You Begin"). The students hear the following conversation:

Paul: Hello?
Joan: Hi, Paul. This is Joan.
Paul: Oh, hi. How are you feeling? Are you still sick?
Joan: No, I feel better, thanks. I'm going to school tomorrow. What's the homework for English class?
Paul: The homework? Just a minute. . . . OK, here it is. Read pages 23 and 24.
Joan: 23 and 24. OK. Thanks. See you tomorrow.
Paul: Bye.

Students listening for gist can easily identify "school" as the main topic of conversation, even though Joan and Paul also discuss the fact that Joan has been feeling sick. They are also able to pick out specific information, in this case, the page numbers for homework. To help learners understand the idea of inference – listening "between the lines" – ask them whether or not both students went to school today. Even though neither speaker directly says that Joan was absent, students can understand that Joan was sick and did not go to class. The key is that students understand what they are listening **for** is just as important as what they are listening **to.**

Many of these ideas are helpful in understanding the listening process, but they should not be seen as rigid models. We need to remember listening is actually very complex. A student listening for gist or inference may, for example, get the clues from catching a couple of specific bits of information.

Remember that although learners need practice in listening, they also need more: They need to learn *how* to listen. They need different types of listening strategies and tasks. They need to learn to preview. Our students need exposure to it all. When learners get the exposure they need, they build their listening skills. They become active listeners.

Marc Helgesen
Steven Brown

Learn how to listen.

FROM THE PEOPLE WHO WROTE THIS BOOK

Dear students:

We hope that you learn a lot of English. We also hope that you enjoy learning it.

There are many different ways to learn. This book will help you learn to listen. Think about how you learn best. Find ways that work for you.

You need to be an active listener. When you listen, do these things:

1. Think about what you are listening <u>to</u>.
   - What is the topic?
   - What do you already know about the topic?
2. Think about what you are listening <u>for</u>.
   - What do you need to know?
   - What do you need to do?
3. When you don't understand, <u>ask</u>.
   - For example, you could say, "Could you repeat that?"

Good luck with learning English. You can do it!

Sincerely,

Marc Helgesen

Steven Brown

LISTENING TASK 1

Could you repeat that?

❏ Work with a partner.
Look at the pictures.
What do you think the students are saying?

❏ Now listen. Were you correct?
Write the sentences.

What do you say when . . .

I. you want someone to say
something again?

Openyourbooks
topage18.

Could you
repeat that?

E_____
m__?

2. you want to hear the tape again?

Once m_____ ,
P_____ .

3. you don't know how to spell a word?

H_____ d__ _____
spell (that)?

4. you want to know a word in English?

H_____ d__ _____
say (that) in English?

3

Types of listening

There are many ways to listen. We listen differently for different reasons.

1 **Listening for the main idea**
Listen to the conversation.
What is the most important idea? Check (✔) your answer.

✔ dinner ☐ a movie ☐ school

Sometimes you don't need to understand everything you hear.
You just want the general meaning.

2 **Listening for specific information**
Listen again.
What are they going to eat? Check (✔) your answer.

☐ hamburgers ☐ pizza ☐ spaghetti

Sometimes you only need to understand certain information.
Ask yourself, "What am I listening for?"

3 **Listening "between the lines"**
Listen again.
Will they go together? Check (✔) your answer.

☐ Yes ☐ No

Sometimes people don't say the exact words.
You can still understand the meaning.

Try it again. Two friends are talking on the telephone.
Each time you listen, think about the information you need.

1 **Listening for the main idea**
Listen. What is the most important idea?
Check (✔) your answer.

☐ going to the doctor   ☐ school

2 **Listening for specific information**
Listen. Which page numbers should she read?
Write the page numbers.

_____ and _____

3 **Listening "between the lines"**
Listen again. Did both students go to school today?
Check (✔) your answer.

☐ Yes   ☐ No

You heard the same conversation three times.
Each time, you listened for different reasons.
Always think about why you are listening.

Meeting new people

❑ Work with a partner.
   Tell your partner about yourself.
   Where are you from? What do you do?
   What do you like?

I'm Ruth. I'm from Taipei. I'm a teacher.

I'm Charles. I'm from Montreal. I like jazz.

I'm Marta. I'm from Mexico City. I like to read.

I'm _____ .

I'm from _____ .

I'm a _____ .

I like _____ .

I don't like _____ .

LISTENING TASK 1

Hello!

You're at a party.
You're meeting Kent and Lisa for the first time.

Kent

❑ Listen to Kent.
What is your part of the conversation?
Check (✔) your answers.

1. ☑ Yes, I'll have orange juice.
   ☐ I'm hungry.

2. ☐ Yes. The orange juice is very good.
   ☐ I like it, too.

3. ☐ Nice to meet you. I am too.
   ☐ Nice to meet you. I'm (*your name*).

4. ☐ I'm a (*your job*).
   ☐ I really like this music.

Lisa

❑ Listen. Now you are talking to Lisa.
What is your part of this conversation?
Check (✔) your answers.

1. ☐ Yes, I'm having fun.
   ☐ I'm hungry.

2. ☐ Nice to meet you. I am too.
   ☐ Nice to meet you. I'm (*your name*).

3. ☐ Yes, the music is really good.
   ☐ I'm from (*your hometown*).

4. ☐ Yes, club soda, please.
   ☐ I like it, too.

In the United States and Canada, people talk about these things when they meet for the first time:

- the place where they are ("This is a great party.")
- the weather ("Nice day, isn't it?")
- something that is the same for both people ("I live on Oak Street, too.")

Are these topics good things to talk about in your country?

Do you . . . ?   Are you . . . ?

❏ Listen. Finish the sentences.

❏ Are these sentences true for you? Circle "yes" or "no."

PERSONAL SURVEY

1. Do you like <u>jazz</u> ?   Yes   No

2. Are you from a _____ _____ ?   Yes   No

3. Do you like _____ ?   Yes   No

4. Do you like _____ ?   Yes   No

5. Are you from a _____ _____ ?   Yes   No

6. Do you like _____ ?   Yes   No

7. Are you a _____ _____ ?   Yes   No

8. Do you _____ _____ ?   Yes   No

YOUR TURN TO TALK

Find someone who. Stand up. Find a partner. Ask one of the questions above. When your partner says "No," ask a different question. When your partner says "Yes," write the person's name next to the question. Then change partners.

Examples

A: Do you like jazz?   A: Are you from a . . . ?
B: Yes, I do. (*Write B's name.*)   C: No, I'm not.
                                        A: Do you like . . . ?

Brothers and sisters

❏ Work with a partner.
Look at the family tree.
How are these people related?
Write the numbers in the circles.

1. husband • wife
2. mother • son
3. father • daughter
4. brother • sister
5. aunt • nephew

6. uncle • niece
7. grandfather • granddaughter
8. grandmother • grandson
9. father-in-law • daughter-in-law
10. brother-in-law • sister-in-law

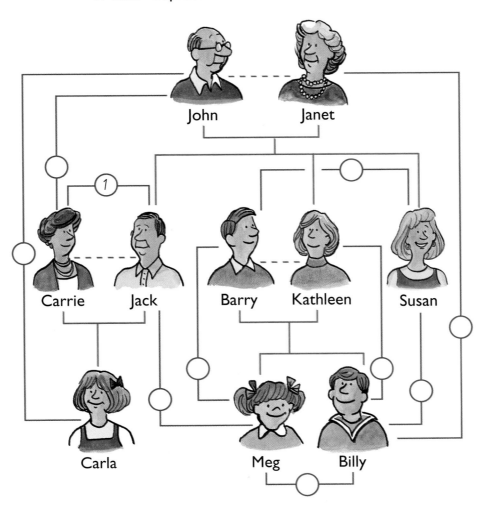

LISTENING TASK 1

Family snapshots

 Listen. People are talking about their families.
Which are the correct pictures?
Check (✔) your answers.

1.

2.

3.

4.

The word "family" means different things in different countries. In some countries, grandparents live with the family. In other places, only children and parents live together. In some countries, children live with their parents until they get married. In others, young people leave their parents' home after high school. Here are average family sizes:

Egypt	4.9 people	Germany	2.3
Korea	4.1	The United States	2.6
New Zealand	3.0		

Who lives together in your country? Do you have a large family?

Your family tree

You're going to write about your family. You need to know these shapes:

star = ☆   square = ▢   diamond = ◇   circle = ○

❏ Listen. Write your answers.

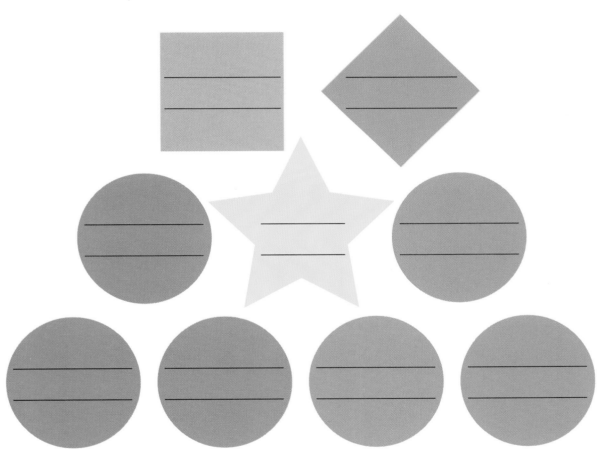

YOUR
TURN TO
TALK

Work in groups of three. Take turns. Tell about the people in your family. Say at least three sentences about each person:

- Where do they live?
- What kind of work do they do?
- What do they do in their free time?
- What do they look like?
- Why do you like them?

Example: My sister lives in Australia. She's a doctor. She plays tennis in her free time. . . .

Numbers

❑ Work with a partner.
Who can count to 100 in English faster?
Begin at the same time. Count as fast as you can. Who won?

❑ Now play the number game. Follow the instructions below.

THE NUMBER GAME

Say these numbers:
- your birthday
- your phone number
- your address
- an important date

Partner, listen and cross out (X) each number you hear. Take turns.

0	1	2	3	4	5	6	7	8
9	10	11	12	13	14	15	16	17
18	19	20	21	22	23	24	25	26
27	28	29	30	31	32	33	34	35
36	37	38	39	40	41	42	43	44
45	46	47	48	49	50	51	52	53
54	55	56	57	58	59	60	61	62
63	64	65	66	67	68	69	70	71
72	73	74	75	76	77	78	79	80
81	82	83	84	85				
86	87	88	89	90				
91	92	93	94	95				
96	97	98	99	100				

Did your partner cross out the correct numbers?
Each correct number = 1 point.

Your points: _____

LISTENING TASK 1

Information

❏ Listen. People want to know the telephone numbers for places in these cities.
Write the telephone numbers.

1. Sydney, Australia
   (02) 266 0610

2. São Paulo, Brazil
   _____

3. Tokyo, Japan
   _____

4. Toronto, Canada
   _____

5. Kuala Lumpur, Malaysia
   _____

6. Mexico City, Mexico
   _____

In the United States and Canada, "100" is used to mean "often" or "many." For example, a parent in the United States and Canada might say to a child, "I've told you 100 times not to do that!" Does your culture use 100 in this way? What are special numbers in your culture?

CULTURE CORNER

13

LISTENING TASK 2
The champions!

❑ Listen. These teams are in a basketball tournament. Write the scores.
Which team wins each game? Write the first letter of the team's name in the circle.

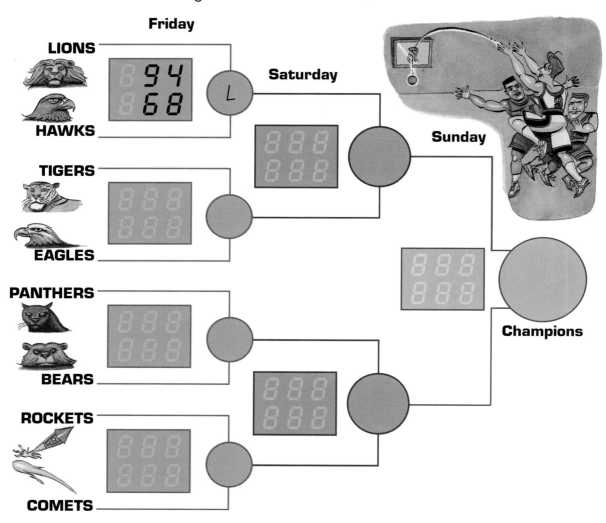

Friday

LIONS

HAWKS

Saturday

TIGERS

EAGLES

PANTHERS

BEARS

ROCKETS

COMETS

Sunday

Champions

94
68

L

YOUR TURN TO TALK

Work in groups of four. How fast can you say your telephone number in English? Take turns saying your number ten times. Say it as fast as you can. Cross out (X) one circle each time you say it. Who was the fastest?

Let's eat!

□ Work with a partner.
These are some of the major food groups.
Write the names in the boxes.

vegetables   fruit   bread and grains
~~meat and fish~~   dairy

□ Do you know the names of the foods?
Write them below.
You can use your dictionary only two times.

FOOD GROUPS

meat and fish

① ② ③ ④ ⑤ ⑥

⑦ ⑧ ⑨ ⑩ ⑪ ⑫ ⑬ ⑭ ⑮

① _steak_
② _____
③ _____
④ _____
⑤ _____

⑥ _____
⑦ _____
⑧ _____
⑨ _____
⑩ _____

⑪ _____
⑫ _____
⑬ _____
⑭ _____
⑮ _____

This tastes great!

❏ Listen. People are eating different foods. They don't say the
   names of the foods.
   What are they talking about?
   Number the pictures (1–6). There are two extra pictures.

☐ pizza   ☐ fish   ☐ sushi (Japanese)

☐ hamburger   1 ice cream cone   ☐ soup

☐ coffee   ☐ nan (Indian)

What foods are popular with young people in your country? What foods don't
most people like? These are the most and least popular foods for teenagers in
the United States and Canada.

Most popular
1. Italian food   5. seafood
2. steak   6. vegetables
3. hamburgers   7. potatoes
4. chicken/turkey   8. Mexican food

Least popular
1. spinach
2. liver
3. broccoli
4. vegetables in general

Do any of the answers surprise you? Which foods do you like and dislike?

16

LISTENING TASK 2

How about a pizza?

❑ Listen. Some friends are deciding where to go to dinner.
Cross out (X) the places where they don't want to eat.
Circle the place they choose. There is one extra place.

Work with a partner. Imagine that you and your partner are going on a picnic. You need to bring something that starts with every letter of the alphabet (except X). Take turns. How fast can you get to Z?

Example

A: You bring the apples. I'll bring the bananas.
B: You bring the bananas. I'll bring the cake. . . .

Your free time

These words tell how often people do things.

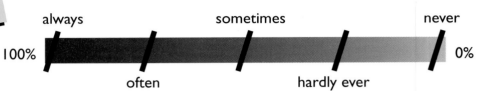

❑ Work with a partner.
How often do you do these things?
How often does your partner do them?
Draw lines.

	you	your partner

How often do you ...

1. read magazines after dinner?

2. play a sport on weekends?

3. study English at night?

4. watch TV on Saturday night?

5. go to a restaurant for lunch?

6. listen to music in the evening?

How often?

❏ Listen. These people are talking about their free-time activities.
How often do they do these things?
Draw lines to show how often.

1. read magazines after dinner

always   never

2. play a sport on weekends

3. study a language at night

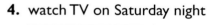

4. watch TV on Saturday night

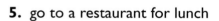

5. go to a restaurant for lunch

6. listen to music in the evening

Some people join clubs for their free-time activities. Clubs are groups of people with the same interests. There are many clubs for sports and music. In the United States and Canada, there are also some unusual clubs. There are even clubs for:

- people who have the same name
- people who love bananas
- people who hate mayonnaise
- adults who like to climb trees

What kind of clubs do people in your country join? Are you a member of any clubs?

CULTURE CORNER

I WANT TO JOIN!

LISTENING TASK 2

Which is more popular?

❏ People in the United States spend their free time in different ways.
Look at the questions. What do you think the answers will be?
Check (✔) your answers.

❏ Now listen. Circle the correct answers.
Write at least one extra fact about each item.

1. Which type of music do more people enjoy?
   ☐ Classical
   ☐ (Country and western)
   ☐ Rock
   Fact: *59 % (like country)*

2. Why do most people listen to the radio?
   ☐ For news
   ☐ For entertainment
   Fact: _____

3. What type of magazines do more people read?
   ☐ TV guides
   ☐ News magazines
   Fact: _____

4. Which sport is more popular?
   ☐ Swimming
   ☐ Jogging
   Fact: _____

5. Which is true of more people?
   ☐ They never exercise in their free time.
   ☐ They like to be active.
   Fact: _____

YOUR TURN TO TALK

Work in groups of about five. Think of a free-time activity. Find out who does it the most. Who does it the least? Stand in a line. The person who does the activity most is first. The person who does it least is last.

Example
A: How often do you listen to the radio?
B: Every day.
C: How about you?
D: Three times a week.

20

That's a nice shirt.

 WARMING UP

❏ Work with a partner.
Do you know the words for these clothes?
Write as many as you can in three minutes.

① *jacket*	⑤ _____	⑨ _____
② _____	⑥ _____	⑩ _____
③ _____	⑦ _____	⑪ _____
④ _____	⑧ _____	⑫ _____

❏ Do you know these designs?
Write the words.

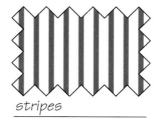

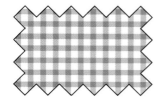

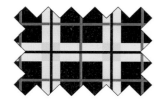

stripes _____   _____   _____

❏ Now change partners.
Read your words. Listen to your partner's
words. Write any new words.

What are they wearing?

❏ Listen. What are Anna and Mike wearing today?
Circle your answers.

Anna

Mike

CULTURE CORNER

Even though people in both the United States and the United Kingdom speak English, they often use different words. Here are some words they use to talk about clothing:

U.S.	U.K.	U.S.	U.K.
cuffs (of pants)	turn-ups	bathing suit	swimming costume
stockings	tights	vest	waistcoat
pants	trousers	sneakers	plimsolls, pumps
suspenders	braces		

Are there any English words for clothing in your language? What are they?

LISTENING TASK 2

Dressing for work

❑ Listen. On Fridays, people in Dan's office wear casual clothes to work. Dan is explaining why. Check (✔) his reasons.

1. With casual clothes ...

❑ People seem friendlier.

✔ Dry cleaning isn't necessary.

❑ People save money.

2. At the office ...

❑ People are more relaxed.

❑ People can work harder.

❑ Less air conditioning is necessary.

3. Getting to work ...

❑ People can ride bicycles.

❑ The trip takes less time.

❑ The clothes are more comfortable for driving.

YOUR TURN TO TALK

Work in groups of three. Look at everyone in the class for one minute. Try to remember what each person is wearing. Now two people close your eyes. The other person will describe what someone is wearing. Try to guess who it is. Take turns.

Example

A: She's wearing a blue sweater.
B: Is it Naomi?

A: No. She's got white shoes on.
C: Is it Maria?
A: Yes, it is.

Furniture and houses

❑ Work with a partner.
These are four rooms in a house.
Write the names in the boxes.

~~bedroom~~   living room   kitchen   bathroom

❑ Do you know the names of the things in each room?
Write them below.

Rooms in a House

<u>   bedroom   </u>

<u>   </u>

<u>   </u>

<u>   </u>

① <u>bed   </u>   ⑤ <u>   </u>   ⑨ <u>   </u>
② <u>   </u>   ⑥ <u>   </u>   ⑩ <u>   </u>
③ <u>   </u>   ⑦ <u>   </u>   ⑪ <u>   </u>
④ <u>   </u>   ⑧ <u>   </u>   ⑫ <u>   </u>

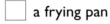

What are they talking about?

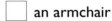

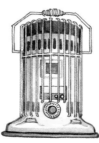

LISTENING TASK 1

❏ People are talking about furniture and other things in houses.
What are they talking about? Number the pictures (1–5).
There are four extra pictures.

☐ a sofa   ☐ a frying pan   ☐ a folding chair

☐ a bed   ☐ an armchair   1 a cabinet

☐ a lamp   ☐ a heater   ☐ an air conditioner

CULTURE CORNER

How big is your house? In the United States and Canada, people usually say, "I have a three-bedroom house" or "I have a two-bedroom apartment." They count the number of bedrooms. This tells you the size of their house. In Japan, people say, "I have a 2LDK" or "I have a 1DK." DK means dining room/kitchen. LDK means living room/dining room/kitchen. The number tells you how many other rooms they have. For example, a 1DK is a small apartment with one room plus a dining room/kitchen. How big is an average house in your country?

Where's the heater?

Around the world, people keep their houses warm in different ways.

❏ Listen. Where are the heaters in these rooms?
Circle them. If there is no heater, check (✔) "none."

1. Syria

☐ none

2. Germany

☐ none

3. Korea

☐ none

4. Brazil

☐ none

5. Japan

☐ none

YOUR TURN TO TALK

Work in pairs. What's your favorite room in your house or apartment? What does it look like? Tell your partner about your favorite room. Your partner will listen and draw a picture of it. Take turns.

Example: My favorite room is the kitchen. I really like to cook. The kitchen is big. There are lots of windows. . . .

How do you start your day?

 WARMING UP

❑ What do you do in the morning?
What do you do first? After that? Number the actions.
~~Cross out~~ the things that you don't do.

☐ I make coffee.

☐ I exercise.

☐ I watch TV.

☐ I read the newspaper.

☐ I eat breakfast.

☐ I listen to the radio.

☐ I take a shower.

❑ Work with a partner.
Read your sentences in order (1, 2, 3, etc.).
Add one of these words to each sentence:
first, then, next, after that, finally.

Example: First, I take a shower. Then I . . .

LISTENING TASK 1

And after that?

❏ Listen to these people. In what order do they do things?
Write the numbers (1–3). There is one extra item for each.

1. What does Eric do in the morning?

☐ He eats breakfast.

1️⃣ He takes a shower.

☐ He listens to the radio.

☐ He reads the newspaper.

2. What does Anne do in the morning?

☐ She watches TV.

☐ She goes to work.

☐ She makes coffee.

☐ She exercises.

3. What does Karen do after school?

☐ She eats dinner.

☐ She watches TV.

☐ She listens to music.

☐ She studies.

4. What does Joel do in the evening?

☐ He eats dinner.

☐ He reads.

☐ He watches TV.

☐ He puts his children to bed.

CULTURE CORNER

Here are some sayings about waking up early:
- "The early bird gets the worm."
- "Early to bed and early to rise makes one healthy, wealthy, and wise."

Do you agree with these sayings? Do you like to wake up early? Does your culture have any sayings like these?

LISTENING TASK 2

And then I . . .

❑ Think about yesterday. What did you do?
You are going to write about your day.

❑ Listen. Write your answers.

1. _____

_____

2. _____

_____

3. _____

_____

4. _____

_____

5. _____

6. _____

_____

YOUR TURN TO TALK

Work in groups of three. Look at your answers to Listening Task 2. Tell your partners what you did yesterday. Use words like these: *first, then, next.* Listen to your partners. How many things were the same?

Example
A: First, I . . .
B: I did that, too.

I'd like to see that!

❏ Work with a partner.
What kind of movie do you like best? Circle it.
What kind of movie does your partner like best? Draw a star (★) next to it.

❏ Write one thing about each kind of movie.
For example: (science-fiction movies)
• something you usually see in that kind of movie (robots)
• the name of a movie (*Star Wars*)
• a famous movie star (Harrison Ford)

Science-fiction movies

robots

Love stories

Action movies

Musicals

Classics

Comedies

LISTENING TASK 1

Let's go!

❑ Listen. Some friends are talking about movies.
Are they going to see the movies together? Check (✔) "yes" or "no."

1. ❑ yes ✔ no

2. ❑ yes ❑ no

3. ❑ yes ❑ no

4. ❑ yes ❑ no

5. ❑ yes ❑ no

6. ❑ yes ❑ no

Some movies are classics. Even though they aren't new, millions of people around the world still enjoy watching them. Some people watch them in theaters. Others watch on video. What are the most popular films of all time? These are the most popular in the United States and Canada:

- *E.T. The Extra-Terrestrial* (1982)
- *Star Wars* (1977)
- *Jaws* (1975)
- *The Sound of Music* (1965)
- *Gone With the Wind* (1939)
- *Snow White* (1937)

Have you seen any of these movies? What movies are "classics" in your country?

Inferring kinds of movies

Understanding evaluations

A night at the movies

Film critics watch movies.
They tell people if the films are good or bad.

❏ Listen. What kinds of movies are the film critics talking about?
Check (✔) them.

❏ Do the critics like the films?
Write "yes" or "no."

THE FILM CRITICS

	Jean	Robert
1. *Beyond the Stars* ☐ horror ☑ science fiction	yes	yes
2. *Another Fine Mess* ☐ comedy ☐ love story	————	————
3. *My Guy* ☐ musical ☐ classic	————	————
4. *Crack Up* ☐ action ☐ comedy	————	————
5. *Just You and Me* ☐ love story ☐ musical	————	————

YOUR TURN TO TALK

Work with a partner. Tell your partner five things about your favorite movie. Use sentences like these:

My favorite movie is _____ .   The movie is about _____ .
It stars *(names of actors)* .   I like it because _____ .

Now work with another partner. Describe your first partner's favorite movie.

Where is it?

❏ Look at these words. Do you know these prepositions?

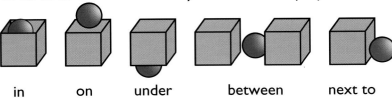

in   on   under   between   next to

❏ Look at the picture for one minute.
   There are many mistakes in it.
   Try to remember the mistakes.

❏ Now work with a partner.
   Close your book.
   What were the mistakes? Make sentences with the
      prepositions and these words:

calendar	coffee table	floor	TV
ceiling	dog	motorcycle	TV stand
chair	fishbowl	sofa	vase

Example: The dog is in the fishbowl.

I'm lost!

❏ Listen. People are looking for places.
   Where are the places? Check (✔) the correct circles.

1. The Four Seasons Restaurant

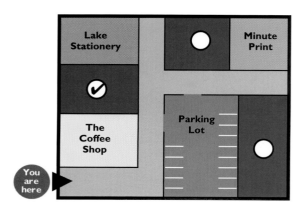

2. The Century Hotel

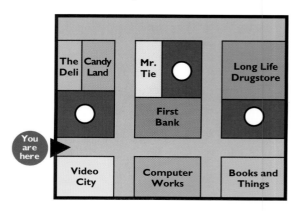

3. a drugstore

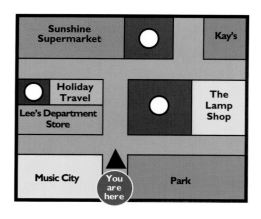

4. a video store

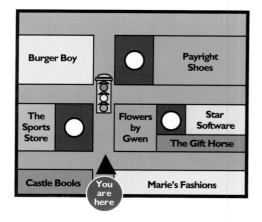

In some languages, people use polite words like "please" when giving directions. ("Please turn right at the corner.") In English, this sounds strange. "Please" is only used for things that help the speaker, not the listener. ("Please tell me how to get there.") Directions are usually given simply. ("Turn right at the corner.") How do you give directions in your language?

Safari Park

Safari Park is a zoo. There are no cages.

❏ Listen to the tour of Safari Park. Where are the places?
Write the numbers on the map (1–6). There is one extra place on the map.

1. The Life Science Center
2. The Brazilian Rain Forest
3. The Children's Zoo
4. Monkey Mountain
5. Lion Land
6. The Gift Shop

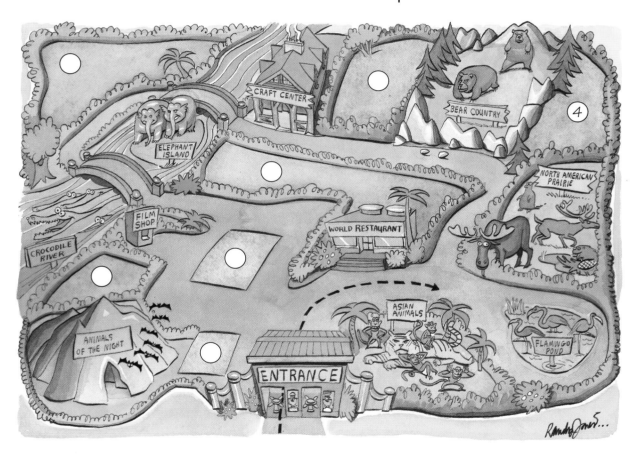

Work in groups of three. Start from your school. Describe how to get from your school to someplace nearby. Partners, draw a map. If you don't understand the directions, ask questions. Who can guess the place first?

Example: Go out the front door. Turn right. Go straight ahead for two blocks. . . .

35

The Midnight Special

You will hear a traditional American song.
The song is about a man. He's in jail.
The Midnight Special is a train.
The man can see it and hear it
from the jail.
He wants the train to take
him to freedom.

❑ Work with a partner.
Match the words to the pictures.

1. to arrest someone
2. bell
3. to gamble
4. Houston
5. pan
6. sheriff
7. straw hat
8. umbrella

☐

1

☐

☐

☐

☐

☐

☐

What's the story?

❏ Listen to the song.
Number the pictures (1–4).

 Folk songs are traditional songs that most people in a country know. They learn the words from their friends and family. Sometimes the words to these songs change over time. Many folk songs have similar topics and words. In American and Canadian folk music, these are some of the most common topics:

- problems with love
- problems with life
- traveling
- jail or prison
- family, especially the mother
- rain
- crying
- hope for the future

Think about folk songs from your country. Are any of the topics the same? What other topics are common?

LISTENING TASK 2
Catch the rhythm.

❑ Listen to the song again.
  <u>Underline</u> the stressed (loudest) syllables.

Oh, <u>let</u> the <u>Mid</u>night <u>Spe</u>cial
<u>Shine</u> a <u>light</u> on <u>me</u>.
Oh, <u>let</u> the <u>Mid</u>night <u>Spe</u>cial
<u>Shine</u> an <u>ever-lov</u>ing <u>light</u> on <u>me</u>.

1. If you ever get to Houston,
   You'd better act right.
   You'd better not gamble,
   And you'd better not fight.
   The sheriff will arrest you.
   He's going to take you down.*
   The next thing you know is
   That you're jailhouse bound.

(Chorus)

2. Every Monday morning
   When the big bell rings,
   You go to the table,
   You see the same old things.
   Not much food on the table,
   Just some bread in a pan.
   If you say anything about it,
   You get in trouble with the man.**

(Chorus)

3. Here comes Miss Rosy.
   Oh, how can you tell?
   By the umbrella on her shoulder,
   She's such a good-looking gal.
   A straw hat is on her head,
   Piece of paper in her hand.
   She wants to see the jailer,
   She wants to free her man.

(Chorus)

* take you down = put you in jail
  This is an uncommon expression.

** the man = the sheriff

YOUR TURN TO TALK

First, sing the song. Then snap your fingers or tap the desk. As a group, read the first verse in rhythm. Try to match the stressed syllables to the rhythm. Finally, work with a partner. Try to read the whole song in rhythm. One person keeps time. (Snap your fingers or tap the desk in an even beat.) The other person reads. Then change parts.

Gifts and greetings

 Work with a partner.
Answer the questions.

Gift Survey

What kinds of gifts do you give when . . .

1. you go to a friend's wedding? _____

2. you visit a friend or stay with
   a family in another country? _____

3. you celebrate a friend's birthday? _____

4. you go to a business meeting? _____

5. you want to give something
   to someone you love? _____

❏ Are there any gifts in your country that have
a bad meaning? Which gifts?

LISTENING TASK 1

Gifts and cultures

People in all countries enjoy gifts.
Sometimes the meanings are different in other cultures.

 Listen. Which item is not a good gift? Cross out (X) the picture.
Why not? Check (✔) your answer.

1. China

✔ A handkerchief means "goodbye."
☐ Dinner costs too much.

2. Argentina

☐ A tie is too personal.
☐ Plants are bad luck.

3. Switzerland

☐ Candy isn't healthy.
☐ Roses mean love.

4. Italy

☐ Even numbers (2, 4, 6, 8, 10) are unlucky.
☐ Odd numbers (1, 3, 5, 7, 9) are unlucky.

5. Japan

☐ Pen and pencil sets are unpopular.
☐ "Four" sounds like the word for "death."

CULTURE CORNER

In many countries, people give special gifts at certain times. Sometimes the customs seem unusual:

- In Australia, a birthday cake for a 21-year-old is often shaped like a key. It means the person is an adult and can come home at any time.
- In parts of Africa, people give a cow as a wedding present.
- Before Korean students take university entrance tests, their friends give them sticky rice candy for luck. The friends hope that the students will pass the test and go to the university.

When do people in your country give gifts? Are there any gifts that people from other countries might find unusual?

LISTENING TASK **2**

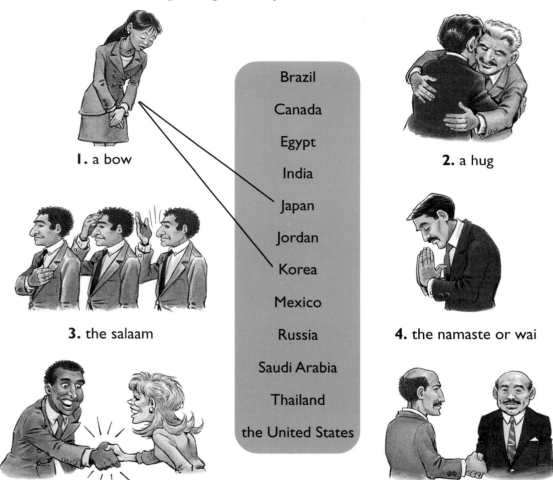

Greetings around the world

❑ Listen. There are many ways to greet people. These are a few examples from some countries.
Draw lines from the greetings to the places. Each has two answers.

1. a bow

2. a hug

Brazil

Canada

Egypt

India

Japan

Jordan

Korea

Mexico

Russia

Saudi Arabia

Thailand

the United States

3. the salaam

4. the namaste or wai

5. a strong, short handshake

6. a softer, longer handshake

YOUR TURN TO TALK

Work in groups of three. What gifts are typical of your country or area? Make a list of five gifts. Then join another group. Combine your lists. Choose the three best gifts. Give opinions like this:

_____ is typical (in my country).

How about _____ ? It's popular (in my country).

Time changes everything.

❑ Work with a partner.
Do you know these jobs?
Write the numbers in the boxes.

1. ambulance driver
2. bodybuilder
3. carpenter
4. factory worker
5. gas station attendant
6. pop musician
7. porter
8. store clerk
9. teacher

☐

☐

☐

☐

1

☐

☐

☐

☐

❑ Now look at the pictures on page 43.
Before they became famous, these people each had one of the
jobs above.
What jobs do you think they had?
Write their old jobs.

LISTENING TASK 1

What did they use to do?

❑ Listen. Did you guess the old jobs correctly?
Correct your answers.

1. Arnold Schwarzenegger
bodybuilder

2. Whoopi Goldberg

3. Walt Disney

4. Michelle Pfeiffer

5. Harrison Ford

6. Bette Midler

7. Sean Connery

8. Cher

9. Clint Eastwood

CULTURE CORNER

In many countries, some entertainers and writers do not use their real names. They use "stage names" (entertainers) or "pen names" (writers):

Stage/pen name	*Real name*
Mark Twain (author)	Samuel Clemens
Ringo Starr (musician)	Richard Starkey
Cher (actress)	Cherilyn LaPiere

Do famous people in your country use stage/pen names? Do you know their real names?

When I was younger ...

☐ Listen. What did you use to do when you were a child?
Write the missing words in the circles.
Then complete the sentences about yourself.

1. When I was a child, I used to (*go to school*) _____ .

2. (_____) , I used to go _____ .

3. (_____) , I used to _____ .

4. (_____) I used to play was _____ .

5. My favorite (_____) used to be _____ .

6. (_____) used to be _____ .

7. (_____) I used to dislike _____ .

8. (_____) I used to like the most was _____ .

YOUR TURN TO TALK

Work with a partner. Read your answers to Listening Task 2. Listen to your partner's answers. Ask at least one question about each answer. Try to learn at least three new things about your partner. How often did you write the same answers?

Example
A: When I was a child, I used to go to school by bus.
B: How long did it take? OR Who did you go with? . . .

Can you describe it?

❑ Look at each word.
Write a word with the opposite meaning.
There is more than one correct answer.

1. right   _____wrong_____ **OR** _____left_____

2. old   _____

3. hard   _____

4. light   _____

5. cheap   _____

6. smart   _____

7. sweet   _____

8. dull   _____

9. narrow   _____

❑ Work with a partner. Play a game.
Say your answers.
Listen to your partner's answers.

• Same word = 1 point.
• Different words with the same meaning
   (*wrong / incorrect*) = 2 points.
• Different words with different meanings
   (*wrong / left*) = 3 points.

Your points: _____

Which one?

❏ Listen. What are the people describing?
Check (✔) the correct pictures.
How did you know? Write the words.

1.

☐   ✔

chocolate, dirty face, cute

2.

☐   ☐

_____

3.

☐   ☐

_____

4.

☐   ☐

_____

5.

☐   ☐

_____

6.

☐   ☐

_____

One of the most common ways to describe something is by its color. But not every language has the same color names. For example, Navaho, spoken by some Native Americans, uses the same word for blue and green. Russian has two words for different kinds of blue: *sinij* and *goluboj*. In English, we also have words for different kinds of blue, like "dark blue" and "sky blue." How many different words for colors do you know in English?

LISTENING TASK 2

Your story

❏ Listen to the story. Imagine the scene.

❏ Listen again. Write the missing words on the lines.
When you hear the bell, write any word in the circle that makes sense.

A (long) road went ___through___ a (⬭) _____ .

A (⬭) _____ was _____ down

the _____ . Suddenly she _____ a (⬭) _____ .

He was _____ a (⬭) _____ ,

(⬭) _____ , and a (⬭) _____ .

He _____ and _____ ,

" (_____) ."

YOUR TURN TO TALK

Creativity Contest. Work in groups of four. Read your stories. Compare the words you wrote when you heard the bell. Whenever someone wrote a word that no one else wrote, he or she gets one point. If everyone wrote different words, each person gets one point. Your points: _____

Finish the story as a group. What happened next?

Languages

Canada

NORTH AMERICA

NORTHERN HEMISPHERE

The United States (U.S.)

Mexico

Pacific Ocean

Atlantic Ocean

EQUATOR

SOUTH AMERICA

SOUTHERN HEMISPHERE

Brazil

WARMING UP

There are probably between 4,000 and 5,000 languages in the world.

❑ Work with a partner.
How many languages can you name in two minutes? Write them.

English _____ _____ _____

_____ _____ _____

_____ _____ _____

_____ _____ _____

❑ Now join another pair.
Read your list.
Listen to theirs.

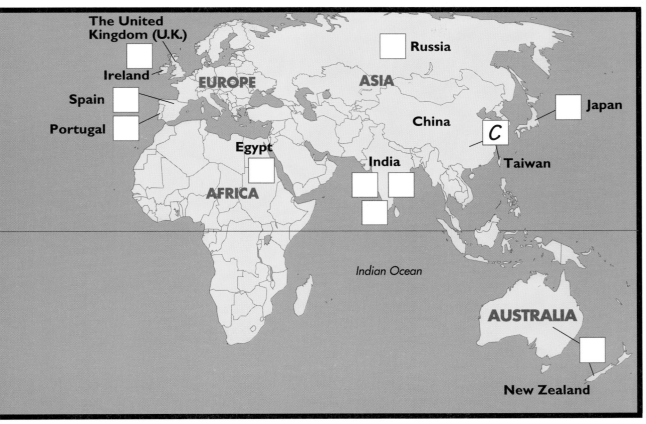

The United Kingdom (U.K.)

Ireland

Spain

Portugal

EUROPE

Russia

ASIA

Japan

China

C

Egypt

Taiwan

AFRICA

India

Indian Ocean

AUSTRALIA

New Zealand

LISTENING
TASK **1**

World languages

❏ Listen. These are the eight languages with the most speakers.
Where do people speak them? Follow the instructions.

Even answering the phone can be different from country to country.

• In the U.S., Canada, the U.K., and Australia, people answer with a greeting: *Hello.*
• In Japan, people say *moshi-moshi.* ("Can you hear me?")
• In Korea, people say *yoboseo.* ("Are you there?")
• Some Spanish speakers say *dígame.* It means "tell me."

Does everyone in your country answer the phone the same way?

49

LISTENING TASK 2
Which English?

❏ Look at the words. Can you tell the difference between American and British English?
Write "A" for American.
Write "B" for British.

❏ Now listen to Chris and Helen.
Chris is from the United States.
Helen is from Great Britain.
Correct your answers.

Chris   Helen

1. [B] lorry
[A] truck

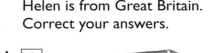

2. ☐ check
☐ tick

3. ☐ crib
☐ cot

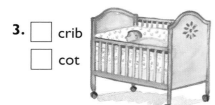  

4. ☐ aubergine
☐ eggplant

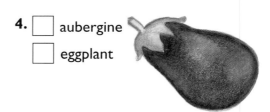

5. ☐ aluMINium
☐ aLUminum

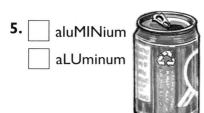

6. ☐ "zee"
☐ "zed"

YOUR TURN TO TALK

Work in groups of four. What languages do you know words in? What are the words? What are the languages? Make a list. Which group has the longest list?

Example
A: "Hello" is *hola* in Spanish. French for "thank you" is *merci*.
B: I can say goodbye in Japanese. It's *sayonara*.
C: "One, two, three, four, five" is *um, dois, tres, cuatro, cinco* in Portuguese.

I like that!

❑ Look at the picture. Think about things you like.
Think about things you don't like.

❑ Work with a partner.
Ask each other questions and fill in the chart.
How many things do you agree on?
Write as many things as you can in five minutes.

WE LOVE . . .		WE LIKE . . .	
_____	_____	_____	_____
_____	_____	_____	_____
_____	_____	_____	_____
WE DON'T LIKE . . .		**WE HATE . . .**	
_____	_____	_____	_____
_____	_____	_____	_____
_____	_____	_____	_____

Example
A: Do you like pizza?
B: I love it.
A: I do too.

 **LISTENING TASK 1**

Same or different?

Sarah

❑ Listen. What things does Sarah like? Check (✔) them.

❑ Do you like the same things? Circle your answers.

1. Places to live ☐ a house ✔ an apartment

2. Food ☐ beef ☐ fish ☐ chicken

3. TV ☐ dramas ☐ news ☐ comedies

4. Vacations ☐ the mountains ☐ the beach ☐ a big city

 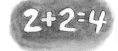 

5. School subjects ☐ English ☐ math ☐ history

 CULTURE CORNER

Many people like to go to other countries on vacation. International travel is popular in most countries. Germans travel the most. In one year recently, three out of every four Germans visited another country. People from the U.S. spend the most money on vacations. Germans are next, and then the Japanese. Where do people from your country go on vacation? Where do you want to go? Is it expensive there?

How about you?

❏ Listen. What do you like to do? What don't you like to do?
Answer the questions with your own ideas.

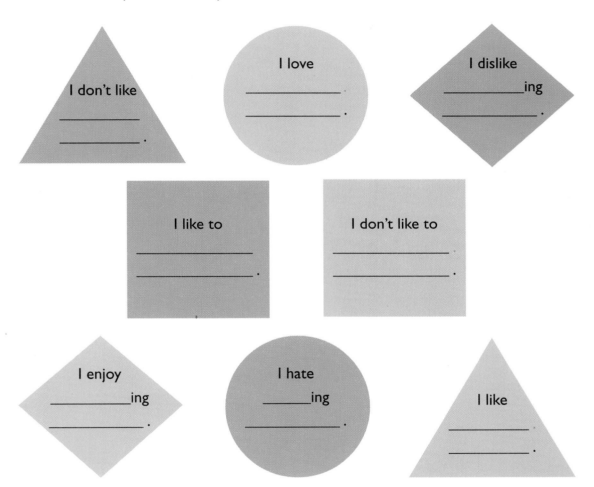

I don't like
_____
_____.

I love
_____
_____.

I dislike
_____ing
_____.

I like to
_____
_____.

I don't like to
_____
_____.

I enjoy
_____ing
_____.

I hate
_____ing
_____.

I like
_____
_____.

YOUR
TURN TO
TALK

Work with a partner. Look at your partner's sentences on this page. Ask about
them. When your partner asks about your sentences, say at least three things about
each.

Example
A: So, you love fish.
B: Yes, I eat it about three times a week.
  My favorite kind is tuna.
  I like it grilled.

53

Strange news

❑ Work with a partner.
These pictures are from an unusual newspaper.
Which words do you think go with each picture?
Write them in the boxes. Some boxes have two words.

~~earth~~	kangaroos	soccer	~~UFO~~
elephant	loses	statue	

❑ What do you want to know about each picture?
Write one question for each.

earth, UFO

1. _____

2. _____

3. _____

4. _____

5. _____

LISTENING **TASK 1**

What ...?!

❏ Listen. What are these stories about?
Write the newspaper headlines.

1. UFO **SENDS** *TV* **SPORTS SHOW TO** *EARTH*

2. GIANT _____ ATTACK _____

3. 2,000-YEAR-OLD GREEK _____ HAS FACE OF _____ _____

4. _____ 100 POUNDS

5. _____ JOINS

In the United States and Canada, several unusual newspapers report strange stories. Many people say they are not always true. These are some of the most popular topics:

- stories about famous people
- UFOs and visitors from space
- strange things about animals
- new diets (ways to lose weight)
- health and medical news
- old rock stars, especially Elvis Presley

Are there newspapers with strange stories in your country? What kinds of stories? Do you believe them?

Do you believe it?

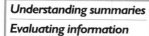
❏ Listen to these stories.
What information is in the stories? Check (✔) your answers.

❏ Do you think these stories might be true?
Draw lines to show your opinion.

True?

Maybe   Probably not   Impossible

1. UFO sends TV sports show to earth.
   ☐ Videotape of UFO sports show found on earth.
   ☑ People on earth saw a TV show from a UFO.
   The show was about sports.

2. Giant kangaroos attack school.
   ☐ The school was damaged, and many students
   were hurt.
   ☐ The school was damaged, but no students
   were hurt.

3. Two-thousand-year-old Greek statue has face of
   rock star.
   ☐ The statue looks like a rock star.
   ☐ The rock star was Greek.

4. Man loses 100 pounds.
   ☐ He stopped eating.
   ☐ He only ate one kind of food.

5. Elephant joins soccer team.
   ☐ The elephant does tricks before soccer games.
   ☐ The elephant is a good soccer player.

YOUR TURN TO TALK

Work in pairs. Think of a very unusual story. Answer these questions:

- What happened?
- Who did it happen to?
- When did it happen?
- Where did it happen?

Now change partners. Ask your partner questions about his or her story. Then
answer your partner's questions about your story.

Holidays

 WARMING UP

❏ Work with a partner.
Think about holidays in your country or other countries.
When do people do the things in the pictures?
Write the name of a holiday for as many pictures as
you can.

go dancing

_____

have fireworks

_____

ring bells

_____

light candles

_____

eat special food

_____

visit relatives

_____

eat candy

_____

go to a parade

_____

remember someone
who has died

_____

❏ How many other holidays can you list?

_____   _____

_____   _____

_____   _____

Fireworks, food, and fun

❑ Listen. People are talking about these holidays.
When are they?
Write the numbers on the correct months. One item has two answers.

1. Martin Luther King Day (U.S.)
2. Moon Festival (China)
3. St. Patrick's Day (Ireland, U.S.)
4. Thanksgiving (U.S.)
5. Thanksgiving (Canada)

6. The Day of the Dead (Mexico)
7. St. Lucia's Day (Sweden)
8. Independence Day (U.S.)
9. Children's Day (Japan)

January	April	July	October
1			
February	May	August	November
March	June	September	December

CULTURE CORNER

In some countries, people make promises on New Year's Day. They say they will change or do something different in the new year. These promises are called "resolutions." Here are the most popular resolutions in the United States:

- Lose weight
- Make or save money
- Stop smoking

- Change something about your job or get a better job
- Exercise more

Do people really change? Some do, but most only keep their resolutions about one month. Less than 20 percent keep them more than two years. Do you celebrate the new year? Do you make "New Year's resolutions"?

LISTENING TASK 2 — Good times

❑ Listen. You will hear about holidays around the world.
Number the pictures (1–4).
Write one more thing about each holiday.

☐ Water Festival

_____

☐ Carnival

_____

☐ Chinese New Year

_____

☐ Kite flying

_____

YOUR TURN TO TALK

Choose a holiday you remember very well. Who were you with? Where were you?
What made the day special?

• Work with a partner. Talk about the holiday for 90 seconds. Then listen to your
  partner for 90 seconds.

• Now change partners. This time, talk for 60 seconds. Listen to your partner.

• Change partners again. This time, talk for 45 seconds. Then listen to your new
  partner. Can you say the same things in only 45 seconds?

Inventions

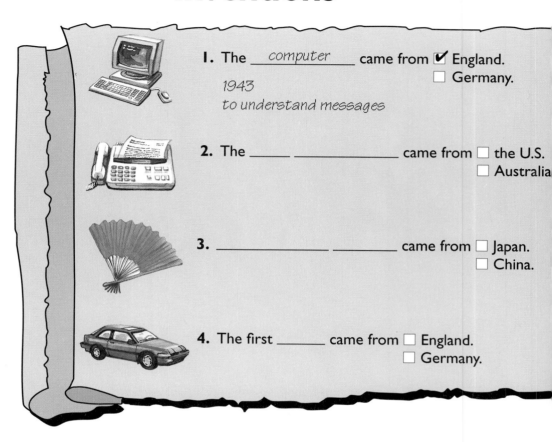

1. The _computer_ came from ☑ England.
  ☐ Germany.
  1943
  to understand messages

2. The _____ _____ came from ☐ the U.S.
  ☐ Australia

3. _____ _____ came from ☐ Japan.
  ☐ China.

4. The first _____ came from ☐ England.
  ☐ Germany.

❏ Look at the pictures on pages 60–61.
  Match these words to the correct pictures.
  Write the words on the lines above.

calendar	clock	folding fans
car	~~computer~~	puppets
chocolate bar	fax machine	

❏ Work with a partner.
  Where do you think these things came from?
  Check (✔) the places.

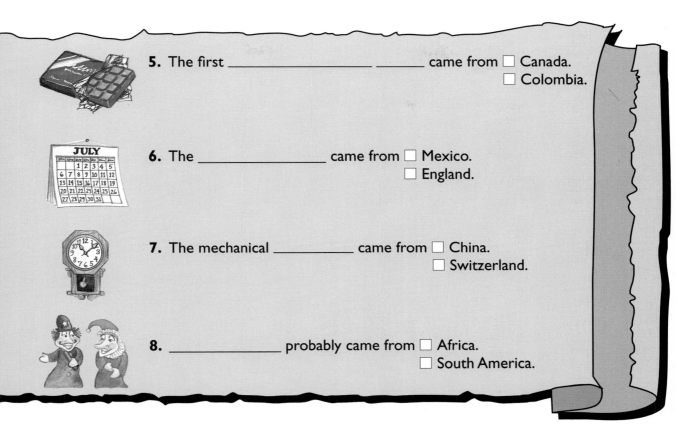

5. The first _____ _____ came from ☐ Canada.
☐ Colombia.

6. The _____ came from ☐ Mexico.
☐ England.

7. The mechanical _____ came from ☐ China.
☐ Switzerland.

8. _____ probably came from ☐ Africa.
☐ South America.

LISTENING TASK 1

Where in the world?

❏ Listen. Were your guesses right?
Correct your answers.
Write one more fact about each invention.

CULTURE CORNER

Many inventions don't come from the places that most people think they do. For example, the first printing press with letters that move wasn't from Germany. It came from Korea in 1234. That's 200 years before the first press in Europe. Most people think the light bulb came from the United States, but Thomas Edison didn't invent it. He just made it better. Sir Joseph William Swan made the first real light bulb in England in 1860. What inventions come from your country?

LISTENING TASK 2

That's really strange!

❑ Listen. These are real products.
What are they used for? Write your answers.

❑ Would you want these items? Which ones? Circle them.

1. These will help keep ___insects___ off you.

2. She bought this to eat _____ .

3. With these mops, your _____ can _____ the floor.

4. She made this to _____ _____ on the train.

5. He uses it to _____ _____ .

YOUR TURN TO TALK

Work in pairs. Imagine you're inventors. You're making a machine. The machine will do something you don't like to do. What will your machine do? What will it look like? Now join another pair. Tell your new partners about your machine.

Example: Our machine is a _____ . We use it to _____ . . . .

UNIT 20

Folktales

Folktales are stories that are very old.
People told them for hundreds of years before anyone
  wrote them down.

❑ Do you know these words?
  Write the words on the picture.

digging   field   ~~treasure~~
farmer   playing   wheat

treasure

❑ Work with a partner.
  You will hear a story that includes the words above.
  What do you think the story is about?

The farmer and his sons

❏ Listen. You will hear a traditional folktale.
Number the pictures (1–6).

In this story, there were three sons. Three is an important number in many folktales. In some stories, people have three wishes. You might know some stories with three: "The Three Goats," "The Three Little Pigs," "The Three Bears." What numbers are important in stories from your country? What other things are important?

The medicine pipe

This story is from North America. The medicine pipe is important for many Native Americans. It was a gift from their god, the Great Maker of All Things.

❏ Listen to the story of the pipe. These words will help you.

winter night
Two men lost their way.
hungry
Something moved.
a woman
food
One man ran.
steal food
fell dead
The other man watched.
The woman looked at him.
put food on the ground
He ate.
The woman sat.
body changed into a buffalo
buffalo changed into a medicine pipe
The man picked it up.
He found his way.
gift from the Great Maker

Randy Jones '95...

❏ Did you like this story?   Yes ☐   No ☐

   Do you know a story like it?   Yes ☐   No ☐

YOUR TURN TO TALK

Work in groups of five. You are going to tell a chain story. It can be a mystery, an adventure story, or a story about magic. One person begins. That person says the first sentence. Start like this:

Once upon a time, *(name)* lived in *(place)* .

Someone else says the next sentence. Each person adds a new sentence to the story. Use some of these words:

two sisters or brothers	a bag of gold	a forest	a bird
an old man or woman	a diamond ring	the moon	fire
a magician	the number "3"	an old house	a teacher

Activation:
a speaking and listening game

The Activation game

- Work in groups of 4.
- Put a marker on "Start here."
- Close your eyes. Touch the "How many spaces?" box with a pencil. Move that many spaces.
- Read the sentences. Answer with at least 3 sentences.
- Take turns.

			How many things can you say when you want someone to repeat something?
			Describe a piece of clothing you bought recently.
			What do you like to do on Sunday?
Start here ➤➤➤	Say three things about every member of your family.	What food don't you like?	Who is your favorite singer? What is your favorite song?
What is your favorite holiday?			
How many kinds of furniture can you name in 1 minute?			Other than this class, where can you hear, read, or use English? How many places can you think of in 1 minute?
Give directions to your favorite restaurant.			*ANY PLAYER CAN ASK YOU ONE QUESTION.*
Imagine you're inventing a machine. What will it do?	Do you know a song in a foreign language? What is it about?	Find 2 things (other than school) that everyone in your group does at the same time.	What is your favorite clothing store? Why do you like it?

Give directions from a well-known place to another place. Don't say where you are going. Partners, guess the place.

Start at . . .

How many languages can you say "thank you" in?

Which holiday don't you like very much?

How many different languages can you name in 1 minute?

Describe your room.

What is the most useful machine you own? Why?

Each person in your group says a number larger than 100. Then, everyone tries to add all the numbers. Who is the fastest?

Name a story that you heard when you were a child.

What is a free-time activity that you used to do often? Choose something that you don't do now.

What is your favorite TV show? Why?

What news story is interesting to you? Why?

Who is your favorite movie star?

What is a typical gift in your culture?

How many spaces?					
2	1	3	1	3	2
1	3	4	2	3	1
3	1	2	1	2	3
1	2	1	3	5	2
3	5	2	1	2	3
2	1	3	4	3	1

YOU CAN ASK ANY PLAYER ONE QUESTION.

In your group, who usually gets up the earliest on weekends? The latest?

What time do you . . . ?

What was your favorite toy when you were a child?

Tell about a good vacation that you've taken.

I went to . . .

What is a food you like but don't eat often? Why?

What is a good movie that you've seen? Why was it good?

I saw . . .

World map

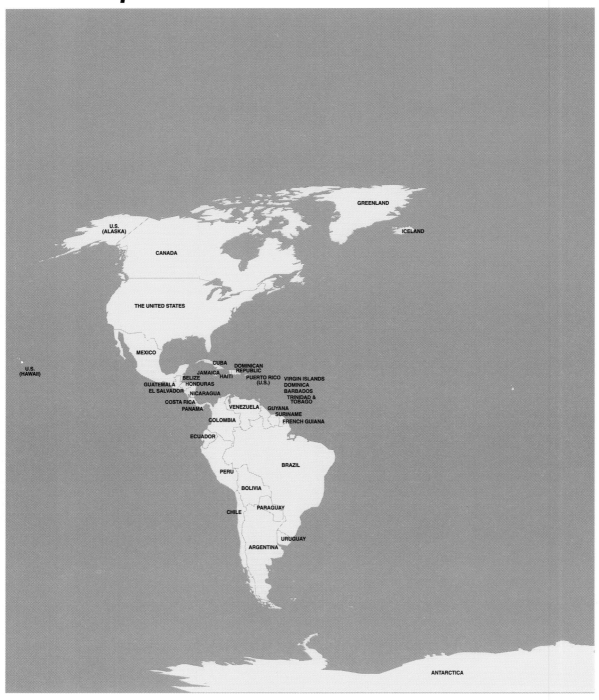

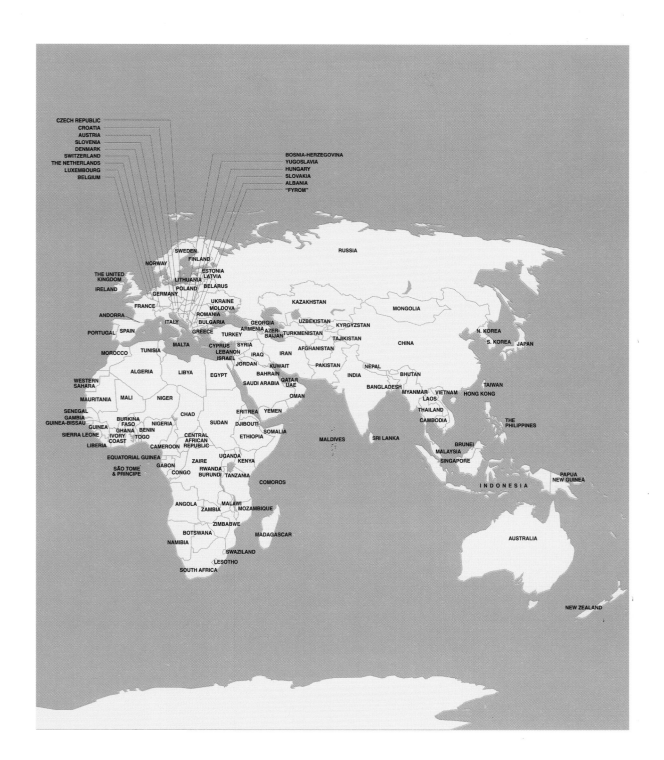

DATE DUE